The Socioeconomic Impact of Injustice

By

Robert Charles Lewis

This book is dedicated to the American ideal of "liberty and justice for all."

Also by same author:

Beyond the Infinite

Poems of Multiple Meanings

Poems of Thoughtful Faith

Writings of Thoughtful Joy

Words of Truth

Developmental Peace

Truisms of Life

Continuing Life

Waterways

Hope

Tests of FAITH

The Quest for Finite Pi

Writings of Muse

Foreword

All injustices detrimentally affect our entire society. Therefore, all people need to be treated correctly at all times. To fairly remedy the socioeconomic problems brought on by all causes, reason must rule over pride, thru the government to the governed. And no earthly government has sovereign immunity, but rather, has sovereign duty to establish, amend, and enforce propitiatory laws. Ergo, we see peace.

Contents

Chapter 1

The Establishment of Law

Law is a needed instrument for all societies in order to establish order and peaceful coexistence.

When law is a true reflection of any society's heartfelt desires, then living in harmony follows.

However, when established law does not satisfy correctly any overall idea of justice commonly held by any group(s) of people within a society, then a "breeding ground" for dissent is formed. From this erupts crime of all sorts, from the petty to the gruesome.

Therefore law in a diversified population becomes ineffective in maintaining peace and order, and also even becomes causal to the increase of crime.

This is shown clearly, as an example, in the United States of America, where crime in many areas has become epidemic. The U.S.A. is a "melting pot" of peoples with cultural and core value differences, that are at times vastly opposed to the status quo of current laws of the land.

Chapter 2

Crime

Crime, by current definition, is the breaking of any established law, whether enforced or not. However, when laws are not just, and also when not equally and uniformly enforced, then technically no crime is committed in the breaking of such laws.

When indeed a particular law is in fact unjust, it needs to be removed from the society wherein it exists, and all who suffered under its enforcement need to be fairly compensated.

Laws that are just need to be enforced uniformly, and all those who break them need to be removed from society, whether it be temporarily or permanently.

Crime should never be rewarded, but rather, admonished.

The allowance of any individual convicted criminal to not do time in a correctional facility only leads to more crime. Word spreads quickly that 'so and so' escaped justice, and this leads many more to willfully commit crime, supposing they too will go 'scot-free'.

And very importantly, law enforcement officers should not feel uncomfortable in themselves being governed by a separate brand of overseeing judges.

"Street justice" is a form of conspiracy to hide the facts from those who are public servants, and neither group should band together in dishonesty.

Chapter 3

The Justification of Law

The very concept of law is to both promote safety and also to help all members of each particular society to live in peace, joy, and contentment.

As it is true that some people do not know their left hand from their right hand, and also that some people do not know right from wrong, it follows that proper laws be formed to provide for every citizen of each society.

A loving and caring enforcement of just laws is key to a successful society.

And no one is exempt from any established law that is both just and even also a foundational basis of a society. I will use as an example what seems as a minor offence, namely jaywalking. Both pedestrians and motor vehicle operators are to blame for some of the most horrific and costly suffering inflicted to the United States of America's citizens.

At intersections where crosswalk lights are placed, at considerable sums of money, pedestrian safety is still not a guarantee. Far too many pedestrians do not obey them and use them properly, and many do not even understand how to use them safely. Coupled with that fact, many motorists will not obey the law either, and thus many injuries occur and also deaths occur needlessly.

It would be very beneficial to our society to put crossing guards at key intersections to promote safety, and also to enforce it.

All motorists and flagrant pedestrians who violate in such situations should be put in a correctional facility in order to instill in them the danger of their actions. This course of action should not be considered as cruel and/or unusual punishment. The loss of one's freedom should be viewed as an educational tool. Operating a motor vehicle is not a right, but rather is a privilege, and any motorist that causes the death of an innocent pedestrian should, by law, lose their privilege to operate a motor vehicle for their entire life.

Justifiable laws are needed in all societies, and people of wisdom must group together to form them and to set in motion the enforcement of them. This is true freedom.

Chapter 4

Poverty

Poverty is the root cause of a large percent of crime in the United States of America. Often people that are unable to afford housing, clothing, and food resort to criminal activity to supply those needs.

The sale of street drugs and thefts, along with armed robberies, and even murders, are the results of impoverished people who have turned to crime to supply their needs.

Once involved in certain types of crimes, most of these 'type' of criminals become truly trapped and entangled with other criminal elements.

Some may be involved with drug lords, some with gangs, and others with pimps and prostitution rings.

With all the monetary blessings bestowed upon the U.S.A., there is an overly ample abundance to eliminate true poverty and all the associated crimes thereof.

Chapter 5

Opportunity

In and of itself, the lack of opportunity to acquire gainful employment that pays a substantial sum to provide a decent living is an example of injustice that can be remedied by simple changes of law.

Minimum wage should be adjusted in all locales to fairly accommodate for cost-of-living variances. This need not necessarily be an hourly wage increase, but also could be accomplished by lowering taxes at all tiers of government, such as Federal, State, City, etc.

To encourage business owners to increase hiring in all situations, tax credits could be used to more than offset any potential risk of net business loss.

Economics can weather any climate of market conditions by simple changes of law.

In not doing proper wage strategies, a governing body is truly derelict in its duty to its citizens. Leaving unemployed people idle leads to social unrest and crime.

Chapter 6

Types of Law

Law has two (2) basic viewpoints.

First is the <u>letter</u> of the law that outlines in writing the specifics.

Second is the <u>spirit</u> of the law that contains the meaning of the words of the law.

The letter of the law is only a rough outline. If not properly understood or enforced, then the law is basically useless and can cause more damage to a society than good.

The spirit of the law is only understood by people of wisdom, and when applied to crime a society benefits thru this form of justice.

There may not always be the letter and the spirit of the law in agreement on a case by case comparison, however the spirit of the law must always prevail in the execution of judgment.

The spirit of the law will always benefit mankind.

Chapter 7

Summary

Injustice has been shown thru-out history to lead to the demise of even great empires. All forms of government likewise will always succumb when they allow unfair, unreasonable, and unjust laws to prevail.

A society that purges itself of wrongful judgment will stand the test of time.

When any particular class of people are singled out by a society and unduly punished, this is a sign of internal rot in the justice system of that society.

When prisons of any nation are overflowing with mostly one type of person, such as creed, color of skin, etc, then even wars can break out.

All societies of mankind are bound by a universal understanding that, in truth, justice does not change in the sense that peace must prevail. Yet there are those bent only on harm and no society can permit this behaviour at all.

Rule of law is a benchmark, however sometimes force needs to be applied to maintain just laws.

Compassion and mercy need to be intertwined with all law.

In ending, there is no earthly compensation capable of healing the damage done whenever even one innocent life is lost to a criminal act.

To solve situational socioeconomic chaos that occurs at times in all societies, there always needs to be calm and wise groups of leaders to amend the initiating root problem, and to solve it, whether by change in law or even simply thru honest education to the masses.

May God bless us all.

Byword:

Ancient Truth

The entire earth, along with all its blessings, are owned exclusively by a higher power, and all we are His children.

We are to share with our brothers and sisters, for in so doing we obey His only law, which is love.

www.ingramcontent.com/pod-product-compliance
Lightning Source LLC
Chambersburg PA
CBHW080404290526
45790CB00009BA/3698